Autism and Me

Autism AND Me

Autism Book for Kids Ages 8–12

An Empowering Guide with 35 Exercises, Quizzes, and Activities!

Katie Cook, BCBA, MEd

ILLUSTRATIONS BY
Cait Brennan

ROCKRIDGE
PRESS

This book is dedicated to Robert, Elizabeth, and Ainsley. I am so proud of you all. Thank you for your love, laughter, and joy.

Contents

A Letter to Kids

Hello and welcome! My name is Katie, and I have joyfully taught children in California for many years. This book is written especially for you, and I'm so glad that you're reading it.

In this book, you're going to learn about autism and what it means for you. But more than that, you're here to really get to know yourself in new ways. Everyone is different, so it's natural that everyone has different skills that are stronger than others. Having autism means that your brain works in a certain way. And that means you'll need to learn specific kinds of skills and strategies that work best for your brain to keep your days moving smoothly. I promise, this is all totally possible if you stick with me and complete the activities in this book. I'll share special tips and tricks to master your feelings, social interactions, self-care, and much, much more.

I'm going to help you every step of the way, and learning together will be fun because we're going to do cool exercises, quizzes, and activities. These will help you discover some of the wonderful reasons to love who you are and what makes you unique. You'll learn more about your strengths and what skills you already have, as well as what skills you may want to develop over time. I know you're going to do great, so let's get started!

A Letter to Grown-Ups

Hello! Thank you for allowing me to help guide your child through understanding their life with autism. Your child is so lucky to have you, and I'm so excited you picked up this book.

This is a guidebook for kids ages 8 to 12 with autism spectrum disorder. The goal is to help them not only understand their ASD but also feel good about themselves in the process. I believe in taking a positive approach when working with children. Frequently pointing out the positive things about having ASD will make your child feel empowered, instead of "less than" or other. Often, books on the market paint ASD as something to "overcome," but this book is meant to take a more positive approach while staying realistic about challenges they may face. ASD is part of what makes your child the unique and the wonderful person they are, but it's not *all* that they are.

The book includes 35 interactive exercises and quizzes to help your child gain the confidence and skills they need to engage with the world around them. These fun activities will also help your child understand their autism better, while learning to embrace the aspects of ASD that are strengths.

All of the exercises, tips, and strategies use evidence-proven methodologies, including Applied Behavior Analysis (ABA) and Acceptance and Commitment Therapy (ACT). ABA is an evidence-based therapy and is considered the gold standard for helping children with autism reach their full potential. There are more than four decades' worth of scientific research supporting the effectiveness of ABA-based procedures to increase meaningful skills for children with autism. Over time, ABA practices have been updated to reflect continuous research and better support children thriving with autism. It's important to always keep researching best practices and solutions for your particular child. The corner-stone of ABA is positive reinforcement, a technique in which reinforcement (like praise) is given to an individual to increase a target behavior or skill.

ACT is a form of behavioral therapy that combines mindfulness skills with the practice of self-acceptance. Strategies that are derived from ACT are based on the idea that thoughts and feelings (private events) influence our behavior (public events). ACT methods help develop psychological flexibility. The goal is for your child to both understand and be more accepting of their thoughts and feelings.

The upcoming chapters follow an organized structure that is designed to be interesting and enjoyable for your child. Each chapter begins with an introduction to a few examples of kids who have ASD. Your child will learn some of their strengths and positive qualities, and then some of the challenges these children sometimes face in their daily lives. After, there are helpful strategies and practical tips to help your child overcome similar challenges. The exercises and quizzes reinforce what is learned in each section, and there's also a section on mindfulness in each chapter, to help your child get in touch with their feelings, manage their emotions, and find calm.

This book is part of a lifelong journey for you and for your child to learn about ASD, overcome obstacles, and, ultimately, celebrate who they are. I'm grateful you have chosen this book along the way.

1

ALL About Autism

It's time to learn all about autism! In this chapter, you'll uncover what being on the autism spectrum means to you and learn about some of the unique things that are happening inside your brain. You'll also investigate how being a kid with autism makes you a very special thinker. It can even be one of your superpowers! Are you ready to get started?

WHAT IS ASD?

What a wonderful question! ASD stands for autism spectrum disorder, but don't let the word "disorder" make you think that there's something wrong with you. In fact, I like to think ASD stands for autism spectrum *difference* instead. That's because being a kid with ASD just means that your brain works a little differently. What does it mean to be "on the spectrum?" Think about a rainbow with its many different colors, all bleeding into each other to create countless color variations. That's how many different kinds of autism there are! Everyone falls at a unique place on the autism spectrum.

A lot of people have different ways they refer to and think about their autism. Throughout this book, we'll just say "ASD" or "autism" to keep things simple, but however you like to identify is fine! No matter what you call it, the bottom line is that you experience the world in a unique way.

Want to hear something really cool? Scientists have machines that take pictures of people's brains and tell us how they work. And guess what they discovered? Each part of the brain has a different job, such as understanding feelings, solving math problems, creating art, or making memories. These scientists discovered that people with autism have certain parts of their brain that are bigger than most people's. Depending on the shapes and sizes of the different parts of your brain, you will have unique, special talents. This might mean that things like science, art, or inventing are much easier for you, but other things, like making friends or controlling your emotions, might be harder.

Now, I'm going to share a very big secret. Look around at the people in your family, neighborhood, and school. Each person is different. We come in all kinds of shapes, sizes, and colors. We all like and dislike different things. We each have our own special talents. This means that being different is normal. It may sound silly, but it's true. So, that's it: The big secret is that **it's normal to be different**. So, finding out what *you're* good at and getting help with the things that are tough for *you* is going to really benefit you in your own unique life.

Getting to Know Me

It's time to learn more about what makes you so special. This is a list of things that kids are sometimes good at. Circle **all** of the things that you are good at.

I'M GOOD AT:

Acting in plays

Art

Asking for help

Being a good friend

Being honest

Being kind

Being quiet

Board games

Brushing my teeth

Building things

Climbing

Compromising

Computers

Crafting

Dancing

Drawing

Following rules

Getting good grades

Helping others

Learning new words or languages

Listening

Making new friends

Math

Memorizing facts

Picking out clothes

Playing a sport

Playing an instrument

Puzzles

Reading

Remembering song lyrics

Remembering numbers

Riding a bike/scooter

Running

Saying "hi" to friends

Saying what I'm thinking

Science

Sharing

Singing

Spelling

Staying calm

Staying in my personal space

Taking a bath

Taking care of animals

Taking things apart

Taking turns

Telling jokes

Telling stories

Understanding facial expressions

Video games

Writing stories or poems

Are there things you are good at that are not on this list? Write them here!

_____

_____

_____

Did you know that some of the things you're really good at are because of your special thinking from ASD? Pretty cool! Thank goodness the world is lucky enough to have more than *7 million* people with autism.

WHAT DOES ASD AFFECT?

Since everyone is different, ASD can affect everyone differently, too. Here are a few common areas of life where ASD might affect you. If ASD does impact you in any of these ways, don't worry! You're going to learn plenty of tips and tricks later to help you along.

Communication: This is how we *share* what we are thinking with other people. Communication can happen with words, faces, or bodies. If you've ever found it hard talking to other kids or understanding what a friend's face means, you're not alone.

Social Interaction: This is *how we act* when we are with other people. For example, people might look at each other in the eyes while talking. When meeting someone new, many people share their name. Some kids with ASD find it helpful to practice these kinds of things.

Self-Care: These are things we do to keep our bodies and brains *healthy*, like taking a shower, brushing our teeth, eating healthy foods, exercising, and thinking positive thoughts. You might have trouble doing these types of things, but it's okay.

Emotions: *Feelings* like happiness, sadness, anxiety, anger, and excitement come from our emotions. If you ever feel like you don't know what do when you have a strong feeling, that's normal.

Family: Some families have mothers, fathers, brothers, sisters, grandpas, or grandmas. Some people find family outside their homes with close friends, teachers, or coaches. No matter who you consider family, family is the *team of people* who love and support you the most. Learning to treat our family with kindness and ask for help is very important.

Autism and Me

Want to get a better idea of the ways ASD might affect you? Circle **all** the answers that apply to you. There are no right or wrong answers!

1. When I talk to a person, sometimes I
   a. forget to look at the other person's face.
   b. don't know how to start the conversation.
   c. talk more than I listen.
   d. forget to ask questions.
   e. None of the above

2. When I am playing with a friend, sometimes I
   a. refuse to share my toys.
   b. forget to say please and thank you.
   c. play only the way I like to play.
   d. leave without saying goodbye.
   e. None of the above

3. When I get up in the morning, sometimes I
   a. forget to brush my teeth.
   b. refuse to eat a healthy breakfast.
   c. think about what will go wrong today.
   d. don't put on clean clothes.
   e. None of the above

4. When I am playing a board game, sometimes I
   a. feel so excited I get up and run around.
   b. feel so angry that I can't finish the game.
   c. feel so happy that I can't control my body.
   d. get confused about what the other players are feeling.
   e. None of the above

5. When I am with my family, sometimes I
   a. don't help with family chores.
   b. refuse to do what I am asked.
   c. know I'm right and will not give in.
   d. get confused, and I don't know how to ask for help.
   e. None of the above

Did you see anything in this quiz you'd like help with? Underline those things. Then keep reading—the next chapters will teach you the skills you need to thrive! When you finish the book, come back to this quiz and see if you can think of a tip or trick that will help with each sentence that you've underlined.

WHY DO I HAVE ASD?

We don't know for sure why some people have ASD and some don't. But many scientists believe that the unique differences in each person's brain come from their genes. So, the special differences in our brains comes from our parents, just like our eye color and height.

Shirley is a girl with autism who is lucky enough to have pictures of her own brain. What she found out by looking at these pictures is incredible. The part of her brain that manages her feelings and emotions is bigger than most people's. She says this is the reason that sometimes she has very strong emotions that are hard for her to control. Another part of her brain is so big that it helps her remember tiny details and create amazingly accurate drawings of what she sees. And guess what—she is now world famous for the wonderful pictures she draws.

Like Shirley, living with ASD gives *you* unique talents, but it can also create challenges to overcome. It's okay to feel down sometimes when things are hard, but remember: ASD is just *a part* of who you are: It's not *all* of who you are. Talking about your feelings can make you feel better. You have lots of people in your life who love you and want to help you.

My Beautiful Brain

Pretend that the picture on the next page is a picture of your brain. Take skills from the Brain Jobs Bank (or make up your own) to fill it in. Put the jobs that you're best at in the bigger spaces, and the jobs that you might want to work on in the smaller spaces.

BRAIN JOBS BANK

Understanding emotions

Learning a lot about a topic

Feeling strong emotions

Understanding faces

Tasting and smelling

Noticing touch and pressure

Seeing the big picture

Remembering numbers and facts

Talking to people

Moving my body

Enjoying music

Solving puzzles and finding patterns

Inventing new things

Building things

Expressing myself through words

Great job! We already learned that every brain looks different, but always remember to celebrate what a unique and beautiful brain you have!

BE MINDFUL

When you're feeling down or overwhelmed, try to "Stop, Drop, and Stroll." Stop what you are doing, drop the negative thoughts from your mind, and take a stroll, or short walk. While on your short walk, think about the things in your life that make you happy and what you're most grateful for. You'll be feeling better in no time!

ASD AND MY LIFE

Your ASD touches different parts of your life because it affects both your brain and your body. It's a part of who you are that is sometimes wonderful and sometimes hard. Here are some examples of places where your ASD may affect you.

At school: One day, you might feel so much excitement in your body that it's hard to stay seated and complete your work. The next day, though, might be amazing because you ace an assignment and make a new friend.

At home: One day, you may have trouble following your morning routine and need extra help getting dressed or brushing your teeth. But the next day you may have an awesome morning after you complete a project that you're proud of.

In the community: One day at the fair, you might be very unhappy with how loud the band is playing their music and need to wear earplugs to lower the volume. Later that evening, you might have a super exciting time riding the fastest rides at the fair.

Strategies in this book will help you navigate all these different situations by tackling each of the areas where ASD impacts your life. In the next few chapters, you're going to find out even more about what parts of your life are positively affected by ASD, and what parts you might want extra help with. Strengthening your skills will help you participate in all the activities that you enjoy the most.

LOVE YOURSELF

Loving yourself is important for a happy life. Reminding yourself about what you are good at is one way to show yourself love and lift your spirits. Look back at the things you circled in the *Getting to Know Me* exercise on page 4. Which three things are you most proud of about yourself?

_____

_____

_____

_____

_____

_____

Knowing Myself Better

You've learned a lot about yourself in this chapter. In this activity, fill in the blanks to create a paragraph that best describes you.

Hi! My name is _____ and I'm _____ years old. I have ASD, which makes me special in many ways. When spending time at home, my favorite thing to do is _____. My favorite thing to do at school is _____. I have many strengths. Three things I'm really good at are _____, _____, and _____. Sometimes I find it hard to _____. One thing I would like to be better at is _____. I am an important part of my family. The thing about myself that I am most proud of is _____.

It's important to focus on the things about ourselves that we are most proud of. It also improves our lives to get help with the skills we want to be better at. This is true for all people! Practice makes progress. Using this book, you can learn to practice the skills that are most important to you.

WHAT DID I LEARN?

Very impressive! You've completed the first chapter in your journey of discovery. Some things you've learned are:

- How having ASD means something different to everyone.

- What ASD means to you.

- What some of your special talents are.

- Which situations are sometimes hard for you.

- The importance of setting goals for skills that you would like to practice.

Next, you will learn valuable strategies for how to practice these skills and approach difficult situations in new ways. Get ready, we're about to have a lot of fun!

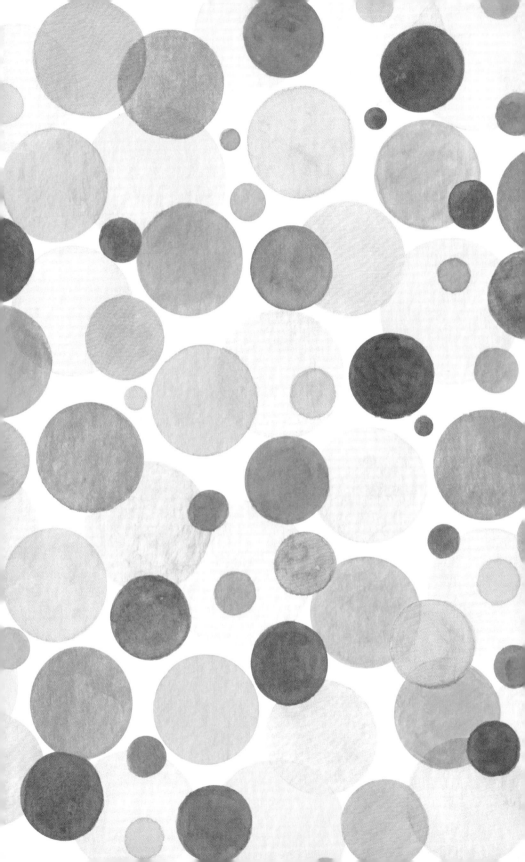

2

ALL About Feelings

Emotions affect how our bodies feel and what we do and say. In this chapter, you'll become an expert in detecting your own emotions, finding out what situations cause which feelings inside you, and learning how *your* body reacts to feeling different emotions. You'll also discover which emotions you want to get better at managing.

REAL KIDS WITH ASD

Meet Sophia. She's eleven years old and very funny, and being at school makes her happy. She especially loves art and science class. When Sophia feels really excited, she interrupts class to tell jokes and make silly noises. She bounces in her seat and gets up to run around the room. Her teacher wrote eight notices home to tell her parents about her behavior. Sophia loves school and doesn't want to get in trouble. She wants to learn how to follow directions and quietly complete her classwork, even when she's feeling excited.

Jacob is twelve years old. Jacob is great with computers and loves playing basketball. But he gets frustrated when things don't go his way. Jacob gets angry when his brother plays with his basketball or goes on his computer without asking. He also gets mad when his mom makes him take a bath. Sometimes, Jacob loses his temper and explodes with his hands, feet, and words. He kicks the wall, pushes his brother, and yells really loudly. Afterward, he feels bad about what he has done. Jacob wishes he knew how to calm down instead of losing his temper.

Keisha is nine years old. She just moved to her grandmother's farm, where there are lots of animals to take care of. Keisha is great with animals, especially horses. But the farmhouse is big and old. Sometimes she imagines things that could happen that make her feel scared. At night, she hides under the covers and tries not to fall asleep. Keisha doesn't like feeling afraid but doesn't know how to stop worrying about spooky things in the dark.

Sophia, Jacob, and Keisha want to be able to manage their behavior when they have strong feelings. Time to play detective! Can you figure out what each one might want to work on?

Friendly Detective

Directions: Review Sophia, Jacob, and Keisha's stories from the "Real Kids with ASD" section. Write one strength that each of them has and one skill that you think they each need to work on. Later in this chapter, you'll learn strategies to help them each understand their feelings and how to control their behavior. You'll also be able to use these tips to increase your own emotional skills.

	Strength	Skill to Work On
Sophia		
Jacob		
Keisha		

UNDERSTANDING FEELINGS

Each day is filled with different situations that will make you feel all kinds of emotions. Have you ever cried or screamed when you were not allowed to play your favorite game? You may have been feeling angry. Have you ever refused to try something new, like join a ball game with friends at recess? You may have been feeling anxious or scared. Knowing what we're feeling is the first step to managing our behavior, so we can have more fun with our friends and family. Here are some tips that will help you recognize your own feelings.

Body Check: Did you know that our bodies give us hints about what we're feeling? If you notice that your hands are fidgeting, you have tingling feelings in your stomach, and your heart is beating quickly, you may be feeling excitement.

Face Check: Our faces also give us clues about what we are feeling. If you detect that your mouth is frowning, your face is hot, and your breathing is heavy, you may be feeling angry.

Events Check: Familiar events will often bring up the same emotions. This means that, if you felt afraid during a certain situation in the past, you might feel scared in that same situation again. If you're unsure about how you're feeling, think about if you have ever been in this situation before and how you felt last time.

EXPRESSING FEELINGS

Once you've mastered understanding *what* you're feeling, you can learn how to *express* your emotions in positive ways. You don't want to keep your feelings bottled up inside, because that makes your body feel uncomfortable, and they may still come out in unexpected ways.

Remember Sophia? When she was excited, she disrupted her class with jokes and funny noises. This got her in trouble. Having ASD makes expressing emotions hard for Sophia. She talked to her teacher about how she felt. They came up with a plan for her to express her excitement with short walks and stretching breaks outside the classroom. It's now much easier for Sophia to control her excitement during class.

Here are a few ideas on how to express your emotions.

Emotions Journal: Write about how you feel and why you think you're feeling this way.

Have a Chat: Talk about how you're feeling with a trusted friend or family member. It can feel good to share your emotions with someone else out loud, even if you don't come up with any solutions.

Move Your Body: Come up with ways to move your body to express your emotions: swim, dance, jump, run, play ball, or more. If you're at school, ask for permission to skip to the bathroom, use a small fidget toy quietly under your desk, or do stretches outside the classroom.

Take a Break: Find a safe, quiet place in your classroom or home where you can sit by yourself if you need to. Stock it with comforting items and headphones or earplugs to block out noise.

If you're not sure how to use these tips yet, that's okay. Don't be afraid to ask your parents or teachers for help. There are many benefits to finding healthy ways to express emotions.

LOVE YOURSELF

In chapter 1, you found out that you've got special talents. Guess what? You can express your emotions through your talents! If you're great at singing or playing a musical instrument, create a song that expresses how you're feeling. It could be a happy or sad song. It's up to you! If you're good at painting or drawing, create a picture that expresses what you're feeling. Making a piece of art can be a great way to express how you are feeling right now rather than keeping your emotions bottled up inside.

Emotions Journal

This journaling practice will help you learn how to express your emotions through writing.

Write about a time that you felt nervous or scared. What were you doing?

_____

_____

How did your face and body feel when you were feeling nervous or scared?

_____

_____

How did you express that you were feeling nervous or scared?

_____

_____

Think about the tips you read about in the "Expressing Feelings" section on page 23. Is there anything you want to do differently to express your feelings the next time you feel nervous or scared?

_____

_____

_____

Color-Coded Feelings

Directions: Everyone feels emotions differently. What happens to your body when you're feeling different emotions? On the following page, color the boxes that show what happens to your face and body when you're feeling happy or excited in *GREEN*. Color the boxes that show what happens when you're angry in *RED*, and finally, color the boxes that show how your body and face feel when you're anxious or scared in *BLUE*. You can color a box two different colors if you feel that way during two different emotions, too.

Once you know what your face and body do when you're feeling strong emotions, use the tips and tricks from earlier in the chapter to express your feelings in positive ways.

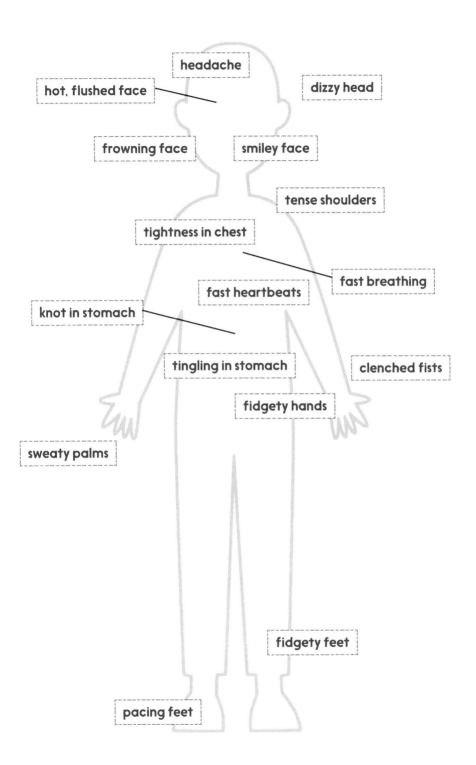

headache

hot, flushed face

dizzy head

frowning face

smiley face

tense shoulders

tightness in chest

fast breathing

fast heartbeats

knot in stomach

tingling in stomach

clenched fists

fidgety hands

sweaty palms

fidgety feet

pacing feet

CONTROLLING NEGATIVE FEELINGS

Knowing how to express negative feelings can be the hardest of all. Feelings like anger, stress, anxiety, disappointment, and sadness can make our bodies really uncomfortable, and it can be difficult to control our behavior.

Remember Jacob? When he's angry, his hands start to sweat, and his heart beats fast. He kicks, pushes, and yells at his family. Jacob is learning new strategies to deal with his anger. He talks about how he's feeling and plays basketball when he feels the need to push or kick something. Doing these things will help *your* body feel good again, too. Here are some other specific tips that can help you.

Don't Take It Out on Others: It's okay to feel upset, but it's never okay to hurt someone else or something that belongs to someone else because of how you're feeling. Use your words to share your feelings nicely. You'll feel better soon, and you'll be glad that you managed your anger and kindly communicated.

Check Your Scales: Imagine that problems and emotional reactions are on a scale of 1 through 10. Does the level of your emotion match the level of the problem? If it's a level 3 problem, like your Dad taking away your favorite toy, your emotional reaction should also be at 3. You can express your anger by respectfully telling your dad why you are angry and taking a walk to cool down.

1 2 **3** 4 5 6 7 **8** 9 **10**
⬆

Use a Calming Strategy: Take slow deep breaths, think about happy things, listen to music, take a walk, slowly count backward from 20, read a book, draw a picture, squeeze a ball, or play with a favorite toy. When Keisha feels scared at night in her grand-mother's big farmhouse, she uses these tips to control her negative emotions. She listens to calming music and looks at pictures in her favorite comic book. Now that she knows how to calm her emotions, Keisha feels more relaxed at night and sleeps much better.

· · · · · · · · · · · · · · BE MINDFUL · · · · · · · · · · · · · · ·

If you're ever feeling upset, try using this visual-ization to calm your mind and body. Think about holding on to a big red balloon. Imagine that the balloon is the problem you are having. Then, let go of the balloon and watch it slowly float away, getting smaller and smaller as it floats high into the clouds. As the balloon disappears, feel peacefulness wash over your body now that the problem is gone.

Your Calming Skills

Practice your skills in expressing your emotions and using calming strategies. What would you do to calm down in each situation?

1. You're going to sleep and feel frightened by a spooky noise. You:
   a. Hide under the covers and try not to fall asleep.
   b. Talk to your mom or dad about how you're feeling, asking them to turn on a night-light and play you calming music as you fall asleep.

2. You're at school and feeling so much excitement that you cannot stay in your seat. You:
   a. Bounce up and down in your seat and try not to get up.
   b. Talk to your teacher and ask her if you can take a break outside to walk and stretch.

3. You're at the park with some friends and feeling sad because they won't play the game you wanted to play. You:
   a. Sit by yourself on the bench and refuse to join the game.
   b. Talk to your friends, ask them to play your game next time, and try to come up with things you like about the game they are playing.

4. You're having dinner with your family and feeling angry because they did not let you eat your favorite meal tonight. You:
   a. Refuse to eat and tell them repeatedly how unfair it is that you didn't get your way.
   b. Talk to your parents about how to earn your favorite meal on Friday and take slow deep breaths as you eat your dinner.

Give yourself **1** point for every **A**, and **3** points for every **B**. What was your score? _____

If your score was 4–6: You'd really benefit from practicing the tips in this chapter and learning to express your emotions positively.

If your score was 8–10: You've got good calming skills. Just keep working on it!

If your score was 12: You have excellent calming skills and are great at expressing your emotions. Way to go!

WHAT DID I LEARN?

You did it! You've completed the second chapter in your journey of discovery. Now you know:

- The importance of understanding your feelings.

- Tips to recognize what you're feeling.

- How to express what you're feeling in creative and productive ways.

- Strategies to control negative feelings and stay calm.

- How to use mindfulness to let go of angry feelings after a conflict.

I am very proud of you for all you have learned about identifying your feelings and expressing your emotions in positive ways. These new skills are sure to help you have great relationships with your friends and family!

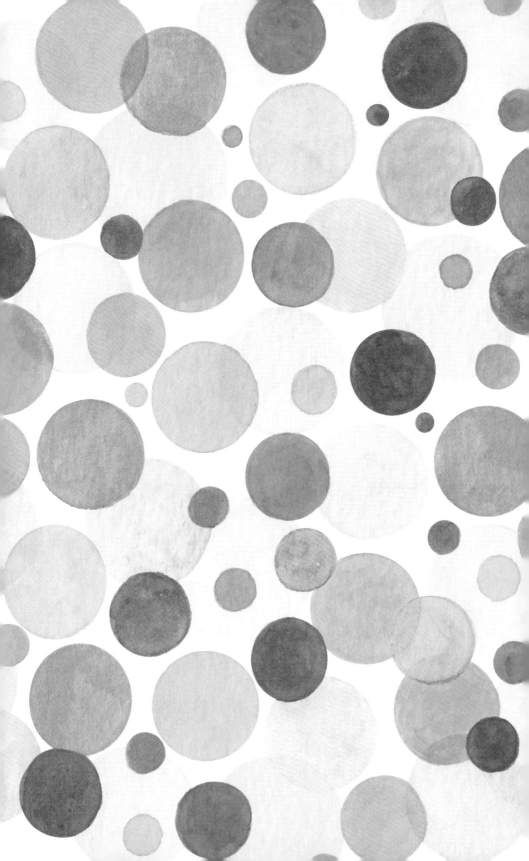

3

ALL About Communication

In this chapter, you'll learn about three main ways people communicate: conversation, body language, and facial expressions. Understanding what other people's faces or body language means can be hard sometimes. Other communication skills, like eye contact and having a two-way conversation, are also things that lots of kids struggle with. But don't worry, you'll learn a bunch of tips on how to communicate what you're thinking.

REAL KIDS WITH ASD

Meet Mateo. He's eight years old and tons of fun to play video games with! He thinks adults are easier to communicate with than kids his age. He's having a hard time trying to talk more with friends at school. He knows how to answer questions, but doesn't know what to ask in return. He also fidgets with his fingers and looks around the room when he talks. Kids sometimes think Mateo isn't interested in talking to them.

Asha is twelve years old. She's bubbly, funny, and really likes to play with other kids. Asha's favorite thing in the world is unicorns. She has no problem walking up to talk to a friend, but she usually talks only about unicorns, which she can talk about endlessly. Asha inches closer and closer to her friends' bodies as she talks, which makes them uncomfortable. Sometimes, they stop talking to her.

Ivan is ten years old and amazing at playing the piano. He puts on big concerts for lots of people. But he has a hard time talking to others. Ivan uses a robotic tone of voice and sometimes hunches over and

looks down when he talks. Other kids don't know what he's saying when he talks this way. At school, Ivan only plays with his sister because it seems like she's the only one who understands him.

Mateo, Asha, and Ivan want to make and keep friends, but their struggles with communication skills are getting in the way. Time to play detective again! Can you figure out what each one might want to work on?

Friendly Detective

Directions: Review Mateo, Asha, and Ivan's stories from the "Real Kids with ASD" section. Write one strength that each of them has and one skill that you think they each need to work on. Later in this chapter, you'll learn strategies to help them each communicate better. You'll also be able to use these tips to increase your own communication skills.

	Strength	Skill to Work On
Mateo		
Asha		
Ivan		

MAKING CONVERSATION

Conversations are like playing a game of tennis. In tennis, people hit the ball back and forth. Just like tennis, a conversation moves back and forth between two people. Sometimes it might be hard to get started or keep the rhythm going. You may not know what to say or ask, and that's okay.

Remember, no one is perfect. Practice makes us all feel more confident. Here are a few tips to get you started.

Ask Questions and Use Fill-In Phrases: It's important to remember to not only answer the questions someone asks you, but also to ask questions back. For example, if someone asks, "What's your favorite ice cream?" you could respond with, "Chocolate. What's your favorite ice cream?" If you're ever unsure what to say next, you can always use a fill-in phrase to keep the conversation going and show that you're interested. You can say, "That's cool," or, "Sounds awesome!" This will give you time to think of what you really want to say. When Mateo began to ask questions and use fill-in phrases during conversations, his friends knew that he was interested in talking to them.

Find Out What You Both Like: Maybe you would like to talk about the solar system all day long. That's okay if the other person loves space, too. However, it's good to find something you both like talking about. When Asha started talking about topics other than unicorns that her friends liked, too, her friends enjoyed talking with her more.

My favorite food is pizza! What's yours?

My favorite food is rice porridge!

Match Your Meaning: Pay close attention to what your tone of voice is "saying." The meaning of words changes depending on *how* you say the words. For example, try saying the words, "Let's go," in a happy way, a sad way, and a mad way. Notice the big difference in looks and sounds each time. When Ivan started practicing matching his voice to the meaning of his words, people were able to understand him better.

BE MINDFUL

Do you ever feel angry or sad when conversations don't go well? It's normal to get upset sometimes. But it's important to take action to calm ourselves down. Here's a cool tip for calming down. Give it a try!

Imagine your breath is your favorite color. Close your eyes and take deep slow breaths in and out, picturing the color that makes you feel happiest. Do this a few times and before you know it, you will be feeling relaxed.

Cool Conversationalist

How are you doing in your journey to become a cool conversationalist? Read each statement and choose how often this has happened to you. Circle your answers.

1. When meeting a new friend, it's easy to think of something to say to start a conversation.
   a. Never
   b. Sometimes
   c. Often

2. When someone talks to me, I stay on the topic they started with by making on-topic comments and asking on-topic questions.
   a. Never
   b. Sometimes
   c. Often

3. I show people that I am interested in what they're saying by smiling, nodding, or making comments like, "That's awesome!"
   a. Never
   b. Sometimes
   c. Often

If you circled **never** for any of the items in this activity, that's a skill to practice. Mateo, Asha, and Ivan struggle with some of the same things. Keep reading, because this chapter is full of tricks and tips to help you learn and grow!

If you circled **sometimes** for any of the items in this activity, that's a skill you already have, but could still use some work. Remember to use the tips you're learning in this chapter.

If you circled **often** for any of the items in this activity, you've discovered what you're best at. Keep up the good work!

BODY LANGUAGE

The way you move, how straight you sit or stand, and how close you are to someone are all a part of body language. For example, if someone crosses their arms, it might mean they are feeling defensive or upset or want to leave. When someone raises their eyebrows quickly, it often means they are very excited or surprised. Sometimes it's tricky to understand what someone's body language is saying. It can also be hard to make your body match what you are trying to say. Here are some tips to make body language easier.

Mirror the Speaker: When talking to someone, try to copy, or mirror, their body language. Mateo saw that his friends keep their bodies still when they're talking to him. Now he keeps his hands in his pockets so he will fidget less with his fingers, and it's much easier for his friends to listen to him.

Keep Your Space: Personal space is how close or far you stand from someone. When talking to a friend, imagine that there's a Hula-Hoop around your body. Try to stand a Hula-Hoop distance away from others when you talk to them. Sometimes people feel uncomfortable if you're too close to them. Asha tried this with her friends, and they all enjoy talking so much more.

Straight and Steady: Standing or sitting up tall lets others know that you want to talk to them. Also, not moving your body too much and looking at the person speaking makes them feel like you're listening to them. Ivan practiced keeping his body still and looking at his friends' faces when he talks to them, and it helped.

LOVE YOURSELF

Are you good at focusing on small details? Do you see the little pink roses on your friend's dress? When you hear your brother say the word "basketball," do you imagine a detailed picture in your head of a basketball flying and scoring a basket? When it comes to conversations, this is a great trait to have! Here's how to make it more useful when you're talking with others.

- Compliment your friend's dress. "That's a beautiful dress. The pink roses really stand out!" This comment could start a wonderful conversation about flowers or favorite clothing styles.

- Share what you picture in your head about basketball with your brother. "I love seeing the ball fly through the hoop. Let's go play basketball!" This comment could excite your brother so much about basketball that he's ready to start a game right now.

The Secrets of Body Language

Here's a chance to practice understanding people's body language.

Directions: Draw a line to match the body language to its meaning.

1. Yawning or head down on
   table with eyes closed   Angry

2. Hands on hips and
   tapping toes   Annoyed

3. Hand pressed to mouth,
   making "shhh" noise   Thinking

4. Scratching forehead
   and looking up   Sad

5. Body facing yours, mouth
   quiet and head nodding   Bored

6. Clenched fists or arms crossed,
   furrowed brow   Tired

7. Head in hand, leaning on
   elbow, unfocused eyes   Be Quiet

8. Body hunched over with a
   frown or tearful face   Paying Attention

ANSWER KEY: 1. Tired 2. Annoyed 3. Be Quiet 4. Thinking 5. Paying Attention 6. Angry 7. Bored 8. Sad

Bonus: Which one of the body language descriptions on page 44 lets you know someone is ready to listen and talk to you?

_____

Double Bonus: When you're talking to someone, describe one way you can use your body language to add to the meaning of your words.

_____

_____

The more you use your detective skills to understand body language, the more success you'll have in your conversations. And guess what? Your face is another great way to share what you're thinking during conversations. Let's find out how.

FACIAL EXPRESSIONS

Facial expressions are when different parts of our faces move to show what we're thinking and feeling during a conversation. Look in the mirror and move your face to see what it looks like when you're feeling different emotions. When you're having a conversation, you can try to match your facial expression to how you're feeling and what you're saying to help people understand you. Watching the facial expressions of your friends will help you understand them, too!

Find the Facial Expressions

Take this time to practice understanding people's facial expressions.

Directions: Cut out pictures of faces from magazines or newspapers and paste them on this page to match how each character is feeling. You could also use markers or colored pencils to draw the faces in.

Items Needed:
- Magazines, newspapers, or other items with pictures that can be cut out
- Scissors
- Glue
- Something to write with

Bonus: Use the word bubbles to write what each person might be saying. Be creative!

happy

angry

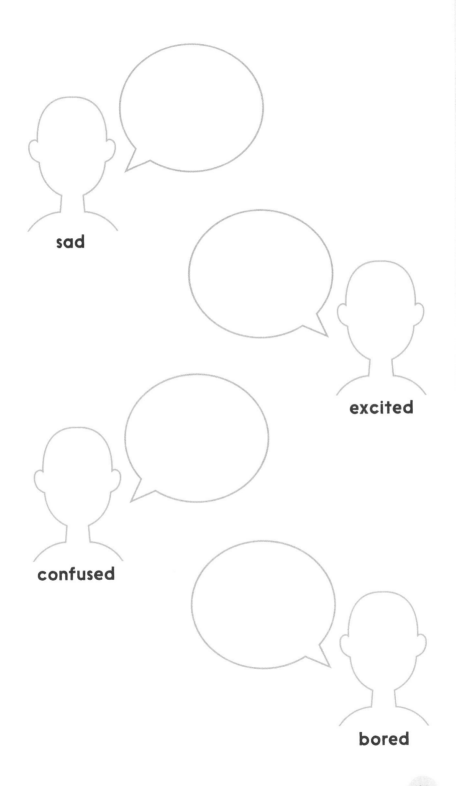

EYE CONTACT

Eye contact is a facial expression that shows you're paying attention to another person. Sometimes it's hard to make eye contact. That's okay. Keep trying, if you're comfortable, and check out the helpful tips that follow.

On the Nose: If eye contact is difficult, focus your eyes on the person's nose or mouth, or look at something right behind them. Mateo practiced looking toward his friends when he talked to them and now has an easier time keeping conversations going.

Check In: Check in on the expressions on other people's faces when you talk to them. Asha used to talk about unicorns without paying attention to her friends' facial expressions. Now she checks in with other people's faces to know if they are losing interest. She's become much closer to her friends now that they have so much more to talk about.

Say Cheese: When talking to someone new, begin by saying, "Hello," with a friendly smile. Smiles help the person you're talking to know to relax and it's proven to help you feel more relaxed, too. Ivan started smiling when talking with his friends. They all felt more relaxed and happy while talking.

WHAT DID I LEARN?

You've finished the "All About Communication" chapter, and you've done a fantastic job!

Here's what we learned:

- Be ready! Practice mindfulness and put on a smile so you're relaxed before talking to someone.

- Watching a person's body or face will tell you more about what they're thinking and saying. You'll know if they're interested in talking right now and if they're enjoying the topic of the conversation.

- Really listening to the person you're talking to will help you stay on topic. If you're not sure what to say next, you can use a fill-in phrase. You can say, "That's cool," or, "Sounds awesome!" This will give you time to think of what you really want to say.

Everyone has their own style of communicating, and we don't always understand each other. If you weren't understood the first time, that's okay. Try to say what you said again in a different way. Remember: The more you practice, the easier communication will be!

4

ALL About Social Interaction

We learned all about communication in chapter 3. Now, we'll build on those skills as we dive deeper into the world of social interaction. You'll learn how to best make and keep friends, share interests and hobbies, and thrive at school.

Don't worry: Understanding how to handle friendships and school is hard for a lot of kids. This chapter is filled with terrific tips and tricks for improving your social skills.

REAL KIDS WITH ASD

Meet Rosa. She's eight years old, very social, and will tell you exactly what she thinks, sometimes in a very loud voice. It's good to be honest, but sometimes what she says hurts her friends and families' ears *and* their feelings. Rosa wants to be a good friend and to join the Girl Scouts at school, but isn't sure how to express herself in a way that doesn't hurt people's ears or feelings.

Andre is twelve years old. This is his first year in a classroom that has no other kids with ASD. Andre doesn't understand why making friends has been hard, but he sits alone at recess and draws incredibly detailed sea creatures. He also gets upset when there are sudden changes in his schedule, like the time the class went to an assembly instead of art time. Andre wishes he could be more friendly and less worried.

Kevin is ten years old and an excellent speller. He won first place in the spelling bee at school. He loves to play word games, and is good at asking his friends to join in. But when they want to play something different, Kevin doesn't like it. What's more upsetting to Kevin is if a subject, like math, is too hard. He hits the table and sometimes

rips up the assignment. He wants to be a good student but isn't sure how.

Rosa, Andre, and Kevin all want to learn new things and enjoy their time with friends at school, but they struggle with different social skills. Time to play detective again! Can you figure out what each one might want to work on?

Friendly Detective

Directions: Review Rosa, Andre, and Kevin's stories from the "Real Kids with ASD" section. Write one strength each of them has and one skill you think that they each need to work on. Later in the chapter, you'll learn strategies to help them with their social skills. You'll also be able to use these tips to help your own social skills, too.

	Strength	Skill to Work On
Rosa		
Andre		
Kevin		

FUN WITH FRIENDS

Friendships are like gardens: The more love and care you give them, the more they grow! Best friends are the kind of friends you can count on to always be there for you and cheer you up when you're sad. You can have lots of other friends, too. These ones you might not know as well and only sometimes spend time with. It's fun to have both kinds of friends.

Empathy: Empathy is when you show someone else you understand how they're feeling. This could be asking a friend if they are okay after they get hurt, or knowing not to joke about their bad hair day. After hearing this, Rosa started to think about how the words she said would make her friends feel.

Sharing Is Caring: Sharing shows friends that you care about them. Try sharing your snack, your toys, or stories about your life. Be careful not to brag. Speaking positively about yourself is good, but when you talk too much about yourself and what you have, friends might feel uncomfortable. Give your friend compliments, too. Andre learned how to make friends by sharing his drawings with them and complimenting their artwork, too.

Give-and-Take: When playing with friends, things cannot always be *your way*. Compromising is when you give a little to get a little back. Make it a goal to do your idea half the time and your friend's idea the other half. Kevin now remembers to compromise with his friends, and they're all happier.

These social skills can be challenging, so just pick one to work on. When it becomes easier, move on to the next. You'll be better at making friends in no time.

BE MINDFUL

Offering a kind ear to a friend means listening to them describe their thoughts and feelings. Having a friend with a kind ear means that they will listen to you share the ups and downs of your day. Be mindful that you have friends with kind ears, and let them know you are also offering a kind ear to your friends. It's a terrific way to reduce stress and feel calm.

Scientists have proven that naming things out loud that are negative helps release their emotional intensity. And naming positive things lets us celebrate together and increases feelings of success. These small moments with friends are very important to our well-being.

Good or Goof

A good friend is someone that you like spending time with. A goof is a tiny social mistake that all people make sometimes. Everyone makes mistakes, but these things aren't nice to do to people. To successfully make and keep friends, you'll need to be a good friend to others. Let's practice what types of social interactions good friends have.

Directions: Read each social interaction and decide if the action is *good* or a *goof*. If it's an action a good friend would do, put a happy face in the box. If it a social goof, put a sad face in the box.

1. Asking a friend what's wrong when they're upset.

2. Talking about yourself all the time.

3. Walking away when asked a question.

4. Talking while a friend is talking.

5. Sharing a treat with a friend.

6. Greeting a friend with a smile.

7. Laughing when others make mistakes.

8. Taking turns picking games to play.

ANSWER KEY: 1. Good 2. Goof 3. Goof 4. Goof 5. Good 6. Good 7. Good 8. Good

INTERESTS AND ACTIVITIES

Everyone has different favorite interests and hobbies. Some kids focus on doing just a few favorite things and become experts. If this sounds like you, it's another thing that makes you special and unique.

It feels great to find other people who enjoy your hobbies, whether they are hobbies you need a group for or hobbies you can do alone. That isn't always easy, though. Here are some tips to get you started.

Pretend Practice: Getting started with a new hobby might be confusing. Before joining a new group, you might try role-playing. Ask your family or teachers to help you by pretending to be the other group members while you practice. This helped Rosa. After she learned all about Girl Scouts, she role-played what she would say and do in a pretend meeting with her sister. Now, she loves her new hobby.

Birds of a Feather: Have you ever heard the saying "birds of a feather flock together"? This means that just as you might see similar birds flying together, people with the same interests enjoy spending time together. But how do you find these people? Ask your parents to help you look for a group to join based on your interests. Start asking the kids at school what their interests are and share yours in return. Andre asked his mom to take him to an art class. He found new friends who also enjoy drawing animals!

Fear Not: It can be scary to try new things. You can decide to face that fear and try anyway. It's possible you won't like it. But what if you decide you love it? You'll never know until you try. Kevin tried many of his friends' hobbies and ended up liking playing tennis.

Trying Something New

Complete this quiz to find out what interests or hobbies you might enjoy.

1. It's easiest for me to learn something new:
   a. By doing it.
   b. By seeing it done.
   c. By listening to someone tell me how to do it.

2. I like to spend most of my time:
   a. Indoors.
   b. Outdoors.
   c. Either indoors or outdoors.

3. I work best:
   a. Quietly by myself.
   b. On a team.
   c. With one or two other people.

4. When it comes to computers, I:
   a. Understand how they work and like them a lot.
   b. Use them mostly just for watching shows and doing schoolwork.
   c. Don't spend much time on the computer.

If you picked mostly **A's**: You might enjoy a hobby like learning computer coding, building or crafting models, creating artwork, or writing stories or poems.

If you picked mostly **B's**: You might be interested in sports like soccer or baseball, getting involved in a group that hikes and learns about nature, or joining a team to practice robotics or chess.

If you picked mostly **C's**: You might like mastering a board game, learning an instrument, joining a drama group, or practicing photography.

What hobbies were recommended for you? Choose a new activity to try out and ask your parent to help you get started.

SCHOOLTIME

All schools, no matter what type, are places where you learn, play, and grow! Learning new things can be tricky, following rules can be hard, and surprise changes can be tough to handle. Here are some suggestions to help make school easier and more fun.

School Rules: Like many other places, schools have lots of rules. But school rules make us, our friends, teachers, and parents much happier. It's easier to follow the rules when you understand them, though, so ask your teacher to explain them. You can also watch your classmates and copy them. Rosa did this and found out she was breaking a school rule with her loud voice. She's trying to use a quieter voice, and her teachers are glad.

Letting Go of Routine: Sometimes the usual school routine changes suddenly. This can make some kids upset. Telling your teacher this bothers you can help, so they can let you know when changes are expected. Unexpected changes might happen anyway, though. Taking deep breaths, slowly counting backward, or playing with a fidget toy can help you stay calm. This way you'll be able to quietly handle it. Andre tries this until he's calm and ready to join the rest of his class when there's a last-minute change.

Get a Helping Hand: Your parents and teachers care about you very much and want to help you succeed.

But they can only help if they know what the problem is. It's important to ask for help. The last time Kevin felt like ripping up an assignment, he asked his teacher for help and explained what he was feeling. She made some small changes to his assignment and offered a little extra time to complete it.

Schooltime Solutions

Directions: Think of something you've struggled with at school. Draw a picture of it here. Then, share more about your experience by answering the questions that follow.

What was the problem?

_____

How did it make you feel?

_____

Which three tips and tricks have you learned that might help solve this problem?

_____

_____

_____

How would you feel if this problem was solved?

_____

_____

Try out your plan and see if it helps solve the problem. Remember, you can ask for help from your parents, teachers, or friends.

WHAT DID I LEARN?

Fantastic job! This was a big chapter, and you finished it. Let's take a quick look at all you have learned:

- Building friendships can feel confusing at times. But you've learned three key actions: empathizing, sharing, and compromising.

- Talking to your friends about how you feel and listening to them is a great way to be more relaxed.

- Hobbies are more fun when you can share them with others. Make it a goal to find kids with interests like your own!

- School is more enjoyable when you practice calming skills and follow the rules. Share your feelings with teachers and parents so they understand your needs and can help you.

5

All About Self-Care

Remember in the first chapter learning that self-care is how we keep our bodies clean and healthy? Well, self-care includes not only our bodies but also the way we interact and think. In this chapter you'll learn about the three main ways people practice self-care: body care and exercise, personal space and boundaries, and positive thinking.

REAL KIDS WITH ASD

Meet Amir. He's eight years old and a great study buddy. Amir likes his classwork, but sometimes plays too rough with his friends at recess. He likes wrestling, which often leads to calling his friends unkind names if things don't go his way. He likes to eat his favorite foods—chicken nuggets and pancakes—all the time, but he doesn't eat any vegetables. He tried broccoli once and didn't like it. Now he thinks all vegetables will taste gross.

Noah is nine years old and loves singing and musicals. He likes to play with friends, but it makes him anxious when people get too close to him. Lately, he has been spending all of his free time alone on his tablet watching videos of his favorite performances. The fact that Noah spends so much time on the tablet makes his auntie, who cares for him, very worried. His auntie wants him to play outside with other kids instead. Being alone so much makes Noah think negative things about himself. He wishes playing with friends didn't make him so anxious.

Lan is eleven years old. She loves reading books and playing the flute. She doesn't love taking showers and brushing her teeth. The smell of the soap gives her a headache, and brushing her teeth is boring. She really likes to hug and stand close to her friends. But the smell from not keeping her body clean is starting to make them stay away, which makes her feel bad about herself.

Amir, Noah, and Lan want to take better care of themselves, but their struggles with completing self-care tasks are getting in the way. Time to play detective again! Can you figure out what each one might want to work on?

Friendly Detective

Directions: Review Amir, Noah, and Lan's stories from the "Real Kids with ASD" section. Write one strength that each of them has and one skill that you think they each need to work on. Later in this chapter, you'll learn strategies to help them each understand self-care better. You'll be able to use these tips to improve your own self-care skills, too.

	Strength	Skill to Work On
Amir		
Noah		
Lan		

BODY CARE AND EXERCISE

Taking care of your body is very important. Eating healthy foods and exercising often keeps you healthy. A clean, bathed body and brushed teeth smell fresh and keep you from getting sick, too. You may not like some of these things, or you might enjoy them very much. Either way, these are daily tasks we all need to do. There is only one you: Take good care of yourself!

Here are a few ideas to make these tasks easier.

Food Fun: You'll be surprised by how many foods you like once you try them! Taking your time with a new food can make trying it easier. Here's a game to play. Make a chart, pick a food, and take the 7-Day Challenge!

Day 1: Look at it.

Day 2: Touch it.

Day 3: Hold it.

Day 4: Smell it.

Day 5: Kiss it.

Day 6: Hold it in your mouth for 10 seconds.

Day 7: Chew and swallow.

Amir began playing this game and has now found that he loves sweet potatoes and tomatoes!

Get Moving: The key to making exercise fun is finding ways to move your body that you enjoy! This could be dancing, playing tag, joining a sport, or walking with a friend. Start slow and work up to spending more time exercising. When Noah put down the tablet and went outside to play, he felt better both inside and out.

Germs, Yuck!: Keep away from bad germs by brushing your teeth, washing your body, and keeping your hands clean. Sometimes kids don't like the taste of the toothpaste, the feel of the toothbrush, or the smell of the soap. Tell your parents how you feel. Once Lan told her mom she didn't like the soap, they found a soap she did like.

Rainbow of Rewards

Routines are actions we do regularly without even thinking about it. Eating healthy, exercising, and washing our hands are easier to do when they are made into routines.

Directions: Pick a few self-care tasks that you would like to do more often. Write the activities on the lines at the start of the rainbow next to **Routines**. After you do them each day, color in the box next to the routine. For example, you may write "dancing" as an exercise activity you will do each day. After dancing on the first day, color in the box under Day 1, next to "dancing." Try to keep up your routine for seven days. Talk to your parents about choosing a reward for completing a week of each task and write the rewards in on the chart.

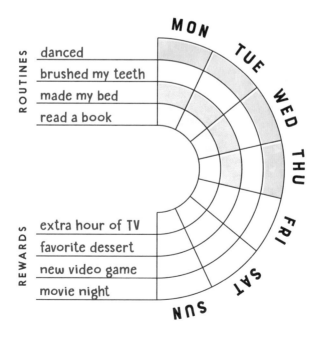

ROUTINES
danced
brushed my teeth
made my bed
read a book

REWARDS
extra hour of TV
favorite dessert
new video game
movie night

MON
TUE
WED
THU
FRI
SAT
SUN

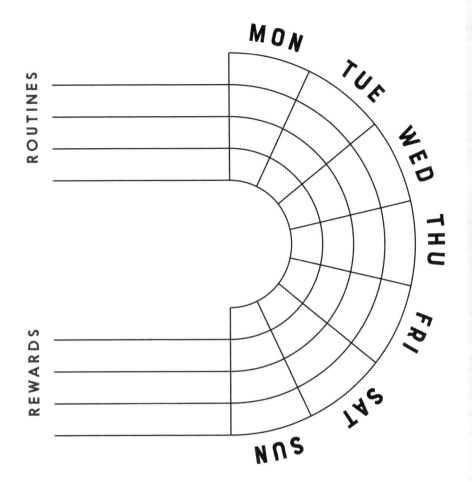

PERSONAL SPACE AND BOUNDARIES

In chapter 3, we talked about how we all wear an imaginary Hula Hoop around ourselves. Our personal space is the space within our Hula Hoop. And the Hula Hoop is the boundary that we don't want people to cross. Everyone's personal space is a different size.

Here are some tips to help you keep those personal space invaders at a distance and to keep you from becoming a space invader, too!

Close Clues: A good social detective is always on the lookout for clues that they are too close to someone. Watch closely for someone moving away from you, pushing you away, or making an unhappy facial expression. Amir and Lan learned to look for clues to know when they might be invading someone's personal space. Once they recognized it and took a step back, they made and kept many more friends.

Ask: If you're ever unsure of what someone's personal space is, just ask, "Am I standing too close?" or, "Am I bothering you?" Listen when the person tells you, "Yes," and take a step back. Speak up when someone is invading your personal space, too. This helped Amir know when wrestling was bothering a friend. Noah began to tell his friends when he needed more space and enjoyed playing more.

Safe Space: We all get overwhelmed sometimes and need extra space. If that happens to you, say, "Excuse me, I need to get some space." Your safe space may be in your room at home or in a quiet reading corner at school. Check in with a trusted adult so they understand your needs and can help you find a good, safe space to relax. Noah has found safe spaces really help him to unwind.

BE MINDFUL: PICTURE PERFECT

Start your morning by picturing in your head how you want your day to go. Right when you wake up, before you get out of bed, picture what you want to happen in your day. Imagine things like following your morning routine, thinking positively about yourself, being a good friend at school, or trying hard during history class. Watch as your great day unfolds a lot like how you imagined it.

Personal Space and Me

Personal space and boundaries are all about choices. Making good choices helps you and others feel more comfortable and play happily together.

Directions: Inside the Hula Hoop, write the numbers of the actions from the list below that are good choices when it comes to personal space.

1. Touching and smelling a friend's hair

2. Talking at a Hula Hoop distance from a friend

3. Kicking someone

4. Saying, "Please move over," if a friend is too close

5. Keeping my body to myself

6. Pulling on a friend's arm to get them to come play

7. Greeting a friend with a high-five

8. Wrestling with a friend after they ask you to stop

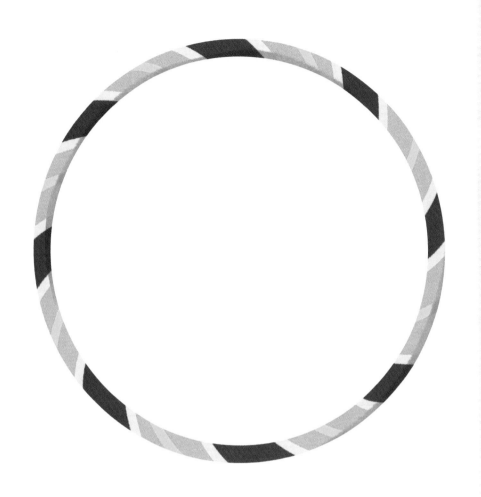

POSITIVE THINKING

Your brain is a very powerful part of your body, and with practice, you can control what it thinks! **Positive thinking** is choosing to think about yourself and the world in a way that makes you feel strong and happy. Keeping your mind open to many different ideas allows you to choose to see the positives in a situation and make good decisions.

Here are some tips that will help you begin using positive thinking.

Think, then Say: Think before you say something. If something you say will hurt another person's feelings, throw that thought away and replace it with a kind thought. Now turn that kind thought into words you can say to someone to make them smile. This helped Amir to replace name-calling words with encouraging and helpful words.

Count the Positives: Look in the mirror. You are special! Now tell your wonderful self all of the things you love about yourself. You can start with, "I love my big brown eyes," or, "I love that my memory makes tests so easy." Pick three positive things to tell yourself each day. Carry them in your head as you go about your day. Feel that positivity! This helped Noah to stop pointing out all of his own mistakes and feel better.

Feel Proud: We all have negative thoughts and feelings sometimes. What helps to keep them away is to do things you are proud of. Whether it's trying out a new morning routine, complimenting a friend, or studying extra hard to pass a test, you'll feel great afterward. Lan decided to use this advice to improve her self-care routine. Once she started bathing and brushing her teeth every day, she felt better than ever about herself.

LOVE YOURSELF

Kids with autism have many unique, special talents. You may be a wiz at solving math problems, a fast runner, a skilled musician, or a creative artist. Make the most of your talents by learning all you can about them so you're always improving. Share your talents with others. This will make others feel great, too. If you feel you haven't discovered your talent yet, don't worry. You will find it. We all have talents. You just need to take a closer look: It's there just waiting for you to find it.

Flying High with Positivity

Some of the phrases on page 79 will lift you *up* and make you feel good. Others just drag you *down* and make you feel upset.

Directions: Color all the phrases on the balloons that show positive thinking. Cross off all the phrases that show negative thinking.

Now take these positive thinking balloons and run with them! Remember, you're in control of your own happiness!

How Positive Am I?

Find out if you're using positive thinking.

Directions: Circle the answer that best describes what you usually think or say.

1. What do you think in your head about yourself?
   a. I can't do anything right.
   b. I'm not as good as everyone else yet.
   c. There are lots of things that are great about me.

2. What do you think or say when you make a mistake or struggle with something?
   a. This is too hard. I give up.
   b. I don't like struggling, I want to do things right all the time.
   c. No big deal, I'll keep trying and do better next time.

3. What do you think or say when a friend doesn't want to play?
   a. No one likes me.
   b. Making friends is too hard for me.
   c. That's okay. I'll just go ask another friend to play.

If you circled mostly **A's**: It's possible that you're being too hard on yourself. Focus on using many of the tips you've learned in this chapter and you'll be thinking positively in no time!

If you circled mostly **B's**: You're almost there. Turn those doubts upside-down by practicing the strategies in this chapter and you'll be flying with positivity in no time.

If you circled mostly **C's**: Way to go! You really know how to focus on the positives and stay happy in life with positive thinking!

WHAT DID I LEARN?

Way to go! You now have the tools you need to become a self-care master. All you need to do is practice! Here's a recap of all that you've learned:

- When it comes to forming healthy self-care habits, finding a way to make the task fun and rewarding will help you keep doing it.

- Always be kind when telling others that you need them to move outside your personal space, and find a safe space if you need a break.

- Don't forget to look for clues that you're the one being the space invader to others. It's important to always be mindful of the imaginary Hula-Hoop we all wear around ourselves.

- Positive thinking is the key to a happy life. There will always be times when you feel like you are struggling to get through the day. But if you use positive thinking, the hard times will be over more quickly.

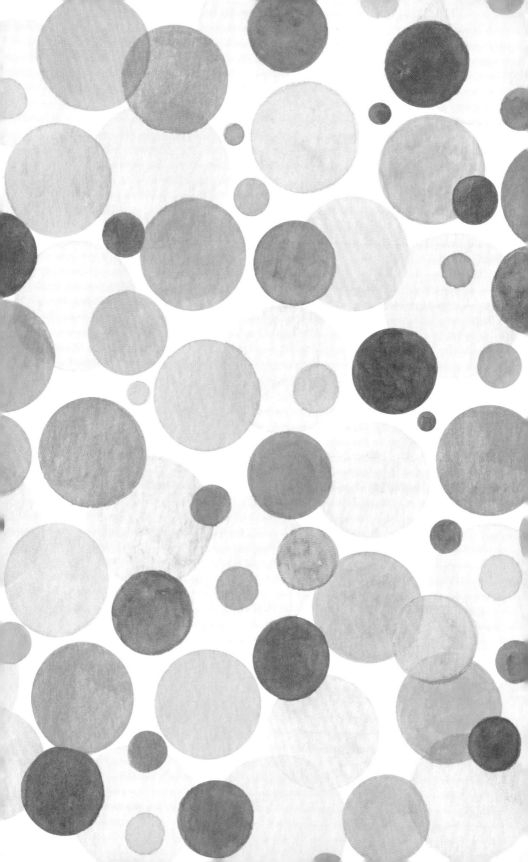

6

ALL About Family

This chapter will be all about the people who are closest to you: your family. Some kids live with lots of family members, others live with just a few, and some even have people they call family that aren't related to them. Even though families may look different on the outside, the core of a family is that they love and support each other. In this chapter, you'll learn how to be a great family team member.

REAL KIDS WITH ASD

Meet Zoe. She's eleven years old and absolutely loves arts and crafts. She often makes special crafts, and her mom hangs them up for everyone to enjoy. Sometimes while crafting, Zoe gets so focused that she empties all of her art supply bins on the floor, and she doesn't put them away. Zoe's mom ends up cleaning up all by herself. Zoe's mom has gotten very frustrated and told Zoe that she's not allowed to do artwork.

Hiro is twelve years old. He's a great baseball player. On weekends, he goes to baseball practice. On weekdays, he plays with his sister. They argue about what they're going to play. Hiro stomps around the house and yells at his sister to play baseball with him. Hiro's dad has told him that if he doesn't get along with his sister, he won't be allowed to play baseball.

Ryan is eight years old and writes fantastic short stories. At dinner, his parents ask him to sit quietly at the table. But Ryan's body feels so full of energy that he can't sit still. He rocks back and forth, flaps his arms, and puts his feet up on the chair. His parents told him that if he

doesn't demonstrate good table manners, he won't get dessert.

Zoe, Hiro, and Ryan want to get along with their families, but their struggles with fairness, conflict resolution, and asking for help are getting in the way. Time to play detective again! Can you figure out what each one might want to work on?

Friendly Detective

Directions: Review Zoe, Hiro, and Ryan's stories from the "Real Kids with ASD" section. Write one strength each of them has and one skill that you think each needs to work on. Later in this chapter, you'll learn strategies to help them each be great family team members. You'll also be able to use these tips to increase your own skills.

	Strength	Skill to Work On
Zoe		
Hiro		
Ryan		

PART OF A TEAM

Being part of a family means being part of a team. On a team, each person has a specific role they play that helps the whole group succeed together. The ideas that follow will help you be a great team member.

Manner Melody: Using good manners and being polite to everyone in your family helps you to have fun together. Here's a poem to help you remember to use manners: "I say thank you and I say please. I never backtalk, scream, or tease. I share my toys and wait my turn. Good manners aren't too hard to learn. It's really easy, when you find: Good manners just means speaking kind."

Home Care: Keeping your home clean and using things carefully to avoid breaking them allows everyone to enjoy the spaces they share. When you take something out, put it away when you're done. Never jump on, climb on, or play on the furniture like a jungle gym. Always clean up if you've spilled something. Zoe learned to do her part to keep her home tidy. She only took out the supplies that she needed and made sure that she cleaned up any messes she made.

Family Fairness: To treat the people in your family fairly means that you should treat others the way you would like to be treated. This includes being quiet when someone is sleeping, taking your turn with chores, and sharing the food at the dining table evenly (yes, even desserts). Taking turns with the computer, iPad, or the TV is another way to be fair. Each person in your family deserves to have their fair chance to sleep, watch shows, play games, and eat.

The Home Team

Directions: Color the parts of the picture that describe being a great team member by *using manners and being polite* YELLOW. Color the parts of the picture that describe being a great team member by *treating your home with respect* **BLUE**. Color the parts of the picture that describe being a great team member by *treating your family fairly* **RED**.

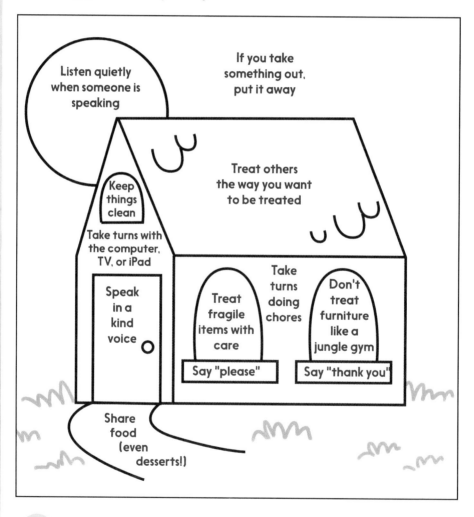

DEALING WITH CONFLICT

A conflict is when two people disagree about something. Sometimes family members have conflicts, and it's important to know how to work through them. Conflict may not be pleasant, but it's not the end of the world. Here are some useful ways to resolve conflicts when they happen with a family member.

Stay Cool: When conflicts arise, it's easy to get angry. Your heart might start pumping, you may begin to yell, and your listening ears might completely turn off. It's impossible to solve a conflict if you're not thinking straight and listening to the other person. To find success in resolving a conflict, first use your favorite calming strategies from chapter 2 (page 30). This will allow you to think clearly and choose the best solution to solve the problem.

Middle Ground: Did you know that compromising is one of the most popular ways to resolve conflict? For example, if your brother wanted to play outside and you wanted to play inside, you could compromise with him by offering to play half the day inside and half the day outside. Hiro found that compromising with his sister was the best way to resolve their conflicts so they could keep playing.

Play Ball: When in a conflict, think of the four bases in a game of baseball. On first base, identify what the problem is. For second base, brainstorm possible

options to solve the problem. When you get to third base, choose how you'd like to fix the issue. Picking a solution that meets the needs of both people in the conflict is sure to get you to home plate. The more you practice, the more home runs you'll have when it comes to resolving conflicts.

BE MINDFUL

Jump out of anger in two minutes. Stand up and do jumping jacks or jump up and down for the first minute. During the second minute, put your hand on your heart and focus your attention on your heartbeat and breathing. It will be fast at first, and then it will begin to slow down. Allow your mind to calm and your strong emotions to decrease as your body's heartbeat and breathing slow down.

The Truth About Conflicts

Directions: Circle whether each statement about conflicts is *true* or *false*.

1. A conflict is when two people disagree about something.
   TRUE **FALSE**

2. Getting upset during a conflict can help you resolve it quickly.
   TRUE **FALSE**

3. Compromising means always getting your way. TRUE **FALSE**

4. Picking a solution that meets the needs of both people in the conflict is the best way to resolve it quicky.
   TRUE **FALSE**

5. Conflicts only happen with people outside your family.
   TRUE **FALSE**

6. Understanding what caused the conflict is an important first step to solving it.
   TRUE **FALSE**

7. To find success when resolving a conflict, stay calm.
   TRUE **FALSE**

8. Most people enjoy dealing with conflict.
   TRUE **FALSE**

9. Compromising is one of the most popular ways to resolve conflict. TRUE **FALSE**

10. Brainstorming possible options to resolve a conflict is no help.
    TRUE **FALSE**

ASKING FOR HELP

One of the best things about having a family is that they can help you, but they may not always know the right way to do that. Sharing how you feel with your family and asking for the things you need will make both you and your family happier. Here are some ideas that will make it easier to ask for help when you need it.

Give Details: Rather than just saying, "I feel angry," or, "I'm sad," you can be more specific about what's going on. For example, when you're feeling very sensitive, you can share that you might cry at any moment. Ryan used this tip to get the support he needed at dinnertime. Once his parents knew how he was feeling, they helped him. Now, Ryan jumps on his trampoline before dinner. Then, he's able to stay still. And yes, he now gets to eat dessert!

Name the Need: After sharing your feelings, tell your family what you need. Needs are different from feelings. For example, you may be *feeling* lonely, but *need* to have some one-on-one time with your dad to feel better. You may be *feeling* frustrated with your brother during a board game, and *need* him to play fairly and follow the rules.

Share with Care: It's important to be kind when sharing your feelings and needs. If you are talking to the person who caused you to feel upset, it's okay to share that with them. Try to tell them in a loving way to avoid hurting their feelings. Share what you need in the form of a respectful request. Asking nicely by saying, "Would you mind doing this?" will go a lot further than demanding, "You must do this!"

LOVE YOURSELF

Remembering successful conflict resolution strategies can help you time and time again. If you have ASD, you may also be gifted with an excellent memory. If this sounds like you, use this skill to your advantage when faced with a challenge. If you're having a disagreement with a family member, try to remember how you solved a similar conflict last time. If it worked before, it's likely the same solution will work again. Focus on the positive ways you have solved conflicts in the past, and you're sure to find success resolving your conflicts in the future.

Help Wanted

Complete this quiz to find out if you know how to ask for help when you need it.

1. Family members:
   a. Stay out of each other's business.
   b. Aren't much help to each other.
   c. Help and support each other.

2. Sharing how you feel with family is best done:
   a. Quickly, to get it over with.
   b. Once you feel better and don't need help anymore.
   c. With details, so they know why you need help.

3. Telling your family what you need:
   a. Is the same thing as telling them how you're feeling.
   b. Doesn't matter, because they won't understand.
   c. Is a big part of getting them to help you in the right way.

4. When it comes to getting help from family:
   a. Make your demands loud and clear.
   b. Don't bother, it's best to handle things on your own.
   c. Sharing kindly and asking respectfully for what you need is a great way to get help and support.

If you picked mostly **A's** and **B's**: You'll want to practice the tips in this chapter so your family will be able to help you during challenging times. Your family loves you and wants to support you when times are tough.

If you picked mostly **C's**: You've mastered the art of getting the help you need from your family. Keep it up! Your family loves you, and they're glad they can help and support you when you need it.

WHAT DID I LEARN?

Amazing! You've finished the last chapter, and you've done an incredible job!

Let's quickly review what we've learned about family:

- A family is like a team, and your role is to be polite by using your manners, treat shared spaces in your home with respect, and treat other family members fairly and kindly.

- Sometimes family members have disagreements. The quickest way to resolve conflicts is to stay calm, look for ways to compromise, and try to find a solution that meets the needs of both people.

- Sharing how you feel with your family and asking for the things you need will make both you and your family happier.

- Focus on the positive ways you have solved conflicts in the past to help solve conflicts in the future.

ACKNOWLEDGMENTS

I would like to express my deepest gratitude to the people in my family. My accomplishments are not my own, but the result of the love and support given to me by family, both the living members and my dearest loved ones who have passed on. They have supported me in every way possible throughout the entirety of my life. The decisions I've made and the life path I've chosen have been guided by the modeling and advice provided by my family. And lastly, the most important events in my life have all been shaped and made possible due to my family's faithfulness, encouragement, and hard work. Thank you all so very much for being in my life.

ABOUT THE AUTHOR

 **KATIE COOK, BCBA, MEd,** is the founder of ATCCOnline.com, an award-winning Applied Behavior Analysis (ABA) training center. Katie provides online Registered Behavior Technician (RBT) certification, eLearning caregiver training, and remote BCBA supervision. Katie is a Board Certified Behavior Analyst and author of the best-selling book *Thriving with Autism*. She has dedicated her professional career to building strategies that bring the entire family into the therapeutic environment for children with ASD. Parent education and caregiver involvement are her passions, and she believes these are the cornerstones of successful ABA programs.